Easy Adult Coloring *Books*

FOR SENIORS BEGINNERS KIDS

: Adult Coloring Books Easy Mandalas

Easy Adult Coloring Books for Seniors and Beginners by Tiny Flowers & Mandalas Books

EASY ADULT COLORING BOOKS FOR SENIORS BEGINNERS KIDS

: Adult Coloring Books Easy Mandalas

Easy Adult Coloring Books for Seniors and Beginners by Tiny Flowers & Mandalas Books

The pages of this book are suitable for colored pencils.
Each picture is printed on one side of pure white paper to minimize scoring and
bleed-through. It is also suitable for framing when complete.

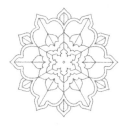

Illustration by Wat Rak, Graphic Elements by Calvin Scott Drews

Made in the USA
Monee, IL
26 February 2023

28714807R00057